Domains of Learning

More than Reading, Writing, and Arithmetic

By Dan Basalone, MS

Copyright © 2024
All Rights Reserved

No part of this book may be reproduced or transmitted in any form or by any means, electronic or mechanical, including photocopying, recording, or by any information storage and retrieval system without the written permission of the author, except where permitted by law.

This book is dedicated to the many educator colleagues with whom I have worked for over 50 years as both an active and retired educator. Special recognition to:

Dr. Marian Fukuda, school psychologist; Dr. Randall Lindsey, professor of education; Dr. Jeanne Fryer, professor of education; Mr. Harry Heppner, school principal; Miss Beverly Mason, school principal; Dr. Michael O'Sullivan, staff development director; Dr. Ruth Valadez, staff development director; Dr. Lillian Utsumi, staff development director; Mrs. Irma Guyton, kindergarten teacher, and Mrs. Patricia McDermott, gifted/enrichment mentor teacher and my aunt. Colleagues have always been the greatest resource in my career development. They all contributed to making teaching one of the noblest of professions.

Table of Contents

Chapter 1 - Overview 1

Chapter 2 - Cognitive Domain 7

Chapter 3 - Psychomotor Domain 9

Chapter 4 - Affective Domain 11

Chapter 5 - Social Domain 14

Chapter 6 - Emotional/Spiritual Domain 21

Chapter 7 - Integrating Domains of Learning 26

Chapter 8 - Conclusion 33

Bibliography 35

About the Author 37

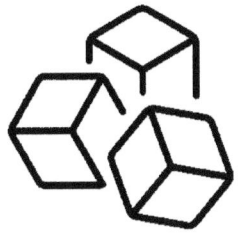

Chapter 1 – Overview

Teaching at its simplest is the mere imparting of knowledge from one person to another. This can be accomplished in many ways including rote memorization, modeling and repetitive practice. However, once knowledge is attained at a certain level of understanding, problem solving begins as does fuller understanding. From my earliest days as a teacher at age 21 to my years as an educator and a reflective retiree, teaching became an ongoing learning process for me. In this book I hope to share my understanding of the true scope of teaching in order for children, our students, to lead successful lives. Lives that not only contain successful and profitable careers, but lives well lived filled with curiosity, satisfaction, kindness, and with love. There is much fear, hate, jealousy and emotional loneliness in society which can be mitigated by learning that teaches students how to make their lives meaningful.

As a beginning classroom teacher, my focus was on presenting lessons that imparted knowledge in a meaningful way. In order to accomplish this task, I was introduced to Madeline Hunter's seven step lesson plan. Every lesson that I taught in my sixth grade classroom had to have an objective, motivation, teacher demonstration, guided practice, student independent practice, independent activity if a student finished independent practice before others, and finally lesson assessment. These seven steps gave me a focus for teaching. What I soon discovered was that motivation was the key to students wanting and needing to learn the lesson. I also discovered that all students learn through differing modality strengths. Some students were visual learners, some were auditory learners, and some needed physical examples. So, the assessment step in the seven step process along with motivation became very important in the learning process.

As you can see, the simple lesson plan became much more complex, and the teacher who could master motivation and assessment were the master teachers. This plan worked very well for the teaching of cognitive skills. However, for skills to become useful the skill also had to bring some joy to the learner. A student can master the skill of reading by learning vocabulary and comprehending meanings, but do they really enjoy reading. Jeanne Fryer, renowned reading educator at UC Riverside, would tell her classes that students truly enjoy reading when they go to a library and select a personal book to read. Therefore, she always recommended that teachers have a classroom library with 50 to 100 books with various themes and levels for students to select in their "free" time. Sharing also becomes important in the selection process because students can gain new interests and insights from peers as well as their teacher. This awareness of the need for enjoyment of learning brought me to my second teaching understanding, the affective domain.

When selecting an objective for planning there are two additional considerations within every lesson plan, vocabulary development and questioning. Every subject in the curriculum has a distinct vocabulary. Without vocabulary knowledge, a student can only have minimal comprehension. Research at the University of Kansas in the field of mathematics identified thousands of words used in the field of mathematics. So, every mathematics lesson is an opportunity to introduce math vocabulary which can be utilized in writing about mathematics or creating math problems. My rule of thumb was to introduce at least five vocabulary words for each subject weekly that were incorporated into a weekly spelling test which included the composition of sentences utilizing the vocabulary either through text or illustration.

The other key lesson component is questioning. The Greek philosopher and teacher Socrates developed the Socratic Method of questioning to encourage higher levels of thinking. Many questions posed during a lesson may be little more than questions that require a yes or no answer. However, higher order thinking skills require higher order questioning; what, where when and who are considered low level questions while how and why questions are considered high level questions. Teachers need to constantly assess their teaching for the quality of their questioning. There is a place for low level questions for basic knowledge and comprehension and high level questions for analysis, synthesis and evaluation.

Motivation was my key to teaching in the affective domain. Children as they mature tend to experience the affective domain constantly by the personal choices that they make. What games will they play? What coloring book do they like? What clothes do they like to wear? What foods do they like to eat? Personal choices have a degree of affect on them. So, in lesson motivation, it was always important to personalize learning as much as possible. It was also important in developing learning activities that personalization was incorporated into the activity. For instance, if students were summarizing a story that they had just read, they could be encouraged to draw an illustration of the story from their perspective. They could create their own mathematics problems based on their learned skill. Much science is based on observation so students could document what they observe in nature from their perspective. Also, teaching games that incorporate learned skills can bring enjoyment to learning.

While my sixth grade class had twenty minutes of physical education each day, I truly learned about the psychomotor domain through coaching a Little League baseball team in my community. The psychomotor domain on the surface seemed explanatory. But, teaching eight-year olds how to play baseball was much more complex. There were basic skills to learn such as throwing, catching and hitting a baseball. These skills require the student/players to observe, imitate what they observed and practice, practice, practice with constant coaching to refine the skills. Much of the motivation and enjoyment came from success. When a player caught a fly ball, threw strikes or got a hit, they were motivated by their success. Of course, success is a great motivator and cause for enjoyment in cognitive learning as well. Success as a motivator can also be found in the social domain and the spiritual/emotional domains as well. As the Little League players got older, bigger and stronger, they learned that in the psychomotor domain taxonomy, they could adapt their skills. For instance, they could throw a curve ball as well as a fastball. They could position themselves in the field in different locations based on the strengths of the batter.

Later in my career as a school administrator, I became acutely aware of the need to fully understand the social domain of learning and the spiritual/emotional domain as well. Schools tend to be a microcosm of society, and as such they teach children how to function positively in society. Concepts such as sharing, kindness, courtesy and respect for others are inherent in a school day. The question then becomes how the social domain is taught. It is not taught in isolation from the other domains, but rather it is an outgrowth of the cognitive, affective and psychomotor domains. All people tend to socialize around something tangible. In school, students engage in learning activities which require socialization skills. For instance the basic skill of listening politely to others. Knowing how to ask questions in a courteous manner. Taking turns during activities. Applauding for others when they have success. As a school principal, one schoolwide goal was a kindness policy. Children, even the youngest, can be taught to use kind words such as "please" and "thank you" appropriately. As students get older, they can understand what empathy means and the importance of random acts of kindness.

Also, as a school administrator working with school psychologists, I learned about the spiritual/emotional needs of students. Spiritual and emotional domain needs tend to be taught in different locations. We normally think of the spiritual domain being emphasized in the family, church, synagogue or temple. While the emotional aspect is found in a school or private setting, spiritual concepts such as love thy neighbor is not only a religious concept but also civic concept. Love of nature is a spiritual concept. Thinking beyond ourselves can be religious or even scientific. Love of self, self-image, is critical for all students to value themselves and others. Therefore, respect for others in the social domain can translate to a positive self-image in the spiritual/emotional domain. This is the domain where language and vocabulary are critically important. Any words that demean another whether through hatred or jest can harm the self-image of another person. Taken to extremes, inappropriate language becomes bullying or hate.

All people at some time in their lives are going to say something or do something that they may regret later or harm someone else. Students in school can be taught ways to make up for an unkindness. When a student does something that is unkind to another student or even their teacher, they can apologize appropriately to that person in order to rebuild respect and self-image for both parties. As a school principal, catching students either in groups or individuals doing something good for others was a daily undertaking. Before leaving school at the end of the day, I would write a complimentary note to the individual or the group to let them know that what they were doing was greatly appreciated. A nurturing environment can become a loving environment. We want students to want to come to school not need to come to school.

As educators, we are indebted to pioneers in learning theory such Madeline Hunter, Benjamin Bloom, and others who have researched and documented the various domains of learning. However, if we are to make their research relevant, it must be put into practice not only in our schools but hopefully in society as a whole through our families. Teaching the taxonomies of learning from lower level skills to higher level skills in each domain is an ongoing challenge for teachers. In the next chapters, I will attempt to further explain the five domains of learning.

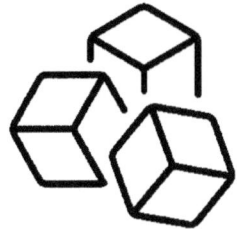

Chapter 2 – Cognitive Domain

In 1956, Benjamin Bloom codified a taxonomy of learning skills for the cognitive domain. Knowledge, comprehension, application, analysis, synthesis and evaluation soon became imbedded in educational lexicon and the planning process for teachers. This hierarchal approach to learning turned from theory into practice. Instead of cognitive learning being mainly a passive, rote activity, it became a thinking and doing process that valued higher order thinking skills rather than just memorization, drill and practice. Students were taught the level skills of critical thinking, creativity and self-evaluation. Of course, as we have seen in recent years in public education with the advent of the politicized standardized test, teacher lesson planning in grades K-12 has regressed in terms of the cognitive learning taxonomy. However quality schools and dedicated teachers are still utilizing the cognitive hierarchy in their planning but with limited planning flexibility.

When teaching, it is critically important to know where you are on the taxonomy hierarchy. One way to remember is what I am going to do in this paragraph right now. Knowledge is remembering facts and figures. Think of knowledge as memorizing the multiplication tables. The next step in the taxonomy hierarchy is comprehension. Comprehension is understanding the knowledge. The next step in understanding the multiplication tables is knowing that multiplication is actually a form of addition and the inverse of division and subtraction. The third step in the hierarchy is application. The skill of applying multiplication for solving. The fourth step in the taxonomy hierarchy is analysis. How can you analyze multiplication to better find uses or convert the multiplication knowledge into algebraic functions. Next is synthesis or creativity. Can you use multiplication in new and creative ways? Can you link the mathematics concept of multiplication to different forms of science like engineering rocketry? And, finally, evaluation, understanding what works and what doesn't.

The common thread through the taxonomy of cognitive, psychomotor and affective domains as stated in *UNLV Online Education, Division of Educational Outreach* is as follows. Lower-level skills within a domain reflect learned knowledge and skills from existing bodies of knowledge. Responses are either correct or incorrect. Higher levels reflect generated meaning and solutions where they are not fixed but explored, negotiated, constructed and valued.

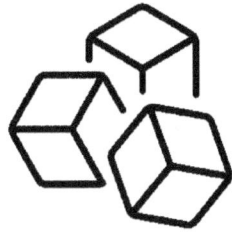

Chapter 3 – Psychomotor Domain

The cognitive domain hierarchy was followed in 1970 (R. Dave), 1972 (A.J. Harrow) and 1972 (E.J. Simpson) by the taxonomy of the psychomotor domain. Physical and perception skills were placed in a hierarchy for teaching purposes. This domain while not as publicized as the prior cognitive domain study was implemented sporadically especially in physical education classes. While many of the domain levels are intuitive such as learning skills by practicing them and then applying them to sports situations, they were never fully implemented broadly by all teachers, especially elementary teachers. In 1970, R. Dave outlined imitation, manipulation, precision, articulation and naturalization as the hierarchy the psychomotor domain. Essentially, the five domain levels took a student from copying a physical skill to repeating the skill independently to mastering the skill for personal use.

In 1972, A.J. Harrow developed a psychomotor domain hierarchy based on muscle development. Reflex movements, fundamental movements, perceptual abilities, physical abilities, skilled movements and discursive communication composed his psychomotor domain hierarchy. Basically, muscles need training to improve from reflex actions and basic movements such as walking and grasping to skilled movements which require muscle development for sports or physical self expression. The highest level could be described as muscle memory.

In 1972, E.J. Simpson developed a psychomotor domain hierarchy that took the basic awareness and proficiency levels to adaptation and origination, the ability to modify and create new movement. In coaching, this is known as learning to play fast. We have all seen the super athlete in any sport who can adapt and make a spectacular play because he or she does not have to overthink the physical task at hand, and we all know that in sports, speed kills. There are sports such as gymnastics, diving and ice skating where new moves are created by individual gymnasts, divers and ice skaters, and the new move is named after them.

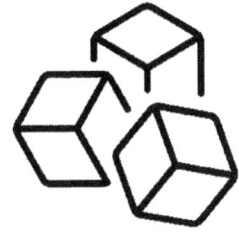

Chapter 4 – Affective Domain

In 1973, D.R. Krathwohl, B.S. Bloom, and B.B. Maria created their taxonomy of educational objectives for the affective domain. This publication recognized that learning required more than just a cognitive or psychomotor curriculum. In order for learning to be internalized, the learner must have a positive attitude toward the object of study. The five affective taxonomy levels are receiving, responding, valuing, organizing a personal value system, and internalizing a value system. Because the affective domain is based on attitudes and beliefs, the question always became how do you measure achievement. The simple answer would be to look at the cognitive data and basically say that if something were learned cognitively to a high degree, the student must be at a high affective level.

But, this is not necessarily true. Many students simply learn in order to get a good grade to please their ego needs or others by getting a good grade on a test. As I stated in the Overview, Dr. Jeanne Fryer, professor of reading education at the University of

California, Riverside, in her lectures on personalized reading would say that you know when a child becomes a true reader when he or she voluntarily selects books to read on a regular basis from an array of choices. Utilizing a learned skill for personal usage or enjoyment is the greatest indicator of an internalized value system

The question for any teacher then becomes how do I plan enjoyment for learning into my lessons. We all know that success tends to breed more success, and success can bring positive reinforcement which affects future success. There is a reason why the Star Wars Trilogy has nine episodes. Most highly successful movies breed sequels. If someone enjoys something, they tend to want more of it. But how do you bring enjoyment during the initial struggle stages of learning a new endeavor? The beginning stages of algebra or biology for instance. One tried and true way to motivate is to refer new knowledge to prior knowledge. A teacher can also show a desired result as motivation. Each discreet subject area has its own unique motivational opportunities. In teaching young students mathematics, it was always helpful to motivate through the use of number games. For initial phonics instruction, rhymes are particularly useful. Just as children can play themselves into reading by perusing picture books, so can they play themselves into becoming mathematicians by playing number games and games with geometric shapes. Many children have learned about real estate and banking from playing the board game Monopoly.

Again, as with the cognitive and psychomotor domain hierarchies, the affective domain hierarchy has fallen prey to the politicized standardized test. Teaching to a test takes the affective "fun" out of learning. Nowadays, it takes an exceptional teacher and understanding school administrators to build affective learning into teaching time constraints. I might also add that limiting music, art and physical education in the curriculum through budget cuts or overemphasis on time for standardized test taking skills will also limit opportunities for teachers to synthesize cognitive lessons with the arts and physical skills such as sports and dance.

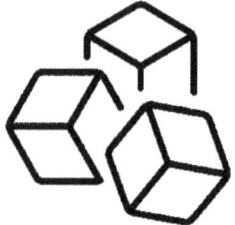

Chapter 5 – Social Domain

Now, we come to a domain that I call one of the two forgotten domains. Teachers have always known that one of the main domains of learning in any school is the socialization process whereby a student enters preschool or kindergarten directly from their family home environment into a heretofore unknown social situation involving other students and adults with whom they have no familiarity. From day one of a child's schooling, socialization is inherent in everything that is taught. I would also submit that quality teaching to higher levels in the cognitive, psychomotor and affective domains requires teaching to higher levels of the social domain. Classroom management and class control are social skills not cognitive, affective or psychomotor skills. Punishing children for misbehavior in a classroom instead of teaching the social skills needed for a cooperative work environment is counterproductive. Think of an adult workplace where workers enjoy each other's company rather than one with jealousy and envy; in which environment would you be the most productive. As with the other domains the taxonomy for the social domain needs to be learned.

I would submit that a taxonomy of the social learning domain would include the following levels: association, courtesy, respect, empathy, random acts of kindness, and ultimately living a life of kindness and goodness. Classroom behavior is always a concern for teachers. They know that it is impossible to teach a group of students at any level without an orderly classroom primed for learning. The question then becomes what social skills are we teaching if the objective is only student discipline and a quiet, orderly classroom. If the student behavior in the classroom under the teacher's direction does not equate to discipline and kindness outside of the classroom, has a social skill really been learned

When students first enter any classroom at any level, they are basically a collection of individuals put together in a loose association due to their proximity to each other in the classroom. Soon, associations breed natural alliances and individual needs. The TV show Big Brother is a good example of individuals in close association learning to work and compete together in a close environment. The difference between the show and a classroom is the objective. In the show the objective is to be the final winner, but in a classroom the objective is for everyone to be a winner. So, the teachers' first responsibility is to find space for the students to associate. This is usually done with seating charts or student selection. If a seating chart is used, the teacher can control the relationships and encourage students to meet others with whom they may not be familiar. If self selection is done, students will tend to gravitate to known rather than unknown students. In younger grades this is usually girls with girls and boys with boys. In older grades it may be by race or ethnicity or common interests like playing on the same sports team.

How a teacher handles student associations can impact social learning. Student associations can also be formed through structured or unstructured group learning activities throughout the day. As a Title I intergroup relations advisor in the Los Angeles Unified School District in the early 1970s tasked with promoting student integration across the city, we utilized shared field trips where volunteer classes in essentially segregated schools were paired for biweekly field trips that were planned by the participating teachers. It was discovered that field trips had to be conducted at least biweekly in order for associations to eventually take place. It was an expensive program, but it was like throwing a pebble in a pond and seeing a ripple effect. I was especially interested in pairings involving student governments in elementary and secondary schools. The student representatives were tasked with sharing what they were learning from the field trip associations back in their schools through their student council class reporting. Socialization can only take place over time which breeds familiarity and understanding.

Once students have become acclimated to their new associations, the next step is the development of courtesy among and between students. We all know that close proximity requires courteous actions whether that means sharing space and materials or taking turns speaking. Learning how to share by asking for something politely is a practiced behavior. Please may I have something and thank you for something are learned behaviors that must be practiced. Every time a student monitor distributes paper or other school resource that is an opportunity for students to vocalize kindness statements. Learning to put objects in correct spaces so as not to impact others is a courtesy. Learning to share space by not touching others is a courtesy. Learning to give polite applause after someone presents information to the class is a courtesy. Of course, learning to follow game rules on the playground or during a sport is a courtesy including the encouragement of everyone during the game and handshake at the completion of the game. Taking turns patiently and sharing are paramount to learning courtesy.

With courtesy can come respect. As students interact during a school day, they are getting to know one another. It is practically impossible to respect someone that you barely know. Respect grows with time during the school year. All of the positive courtesy actions certainly contribute to respect. However, respect requires personal knowledge, so it is critical that students be comfortable sharing personal likes and dislikes in the classroom setting. Demonstrated academic and physical prowess in other domains also contribute to respect.

The United States has always been at its core a multicultural country unlike many countries around the world that tend to be more ethnically homogeneous. Of course with globalization and refugee populations, more and more countries are becoming heterogeneous. The fact of multiculturalism creates another critical need for students to learn more about others so that respect can be developed. Recommended reading for any educator at any level should be *Cultural Proficiency: A Manual for School Leaders* by Lindsey, Robbins and Terrell. Students from differing cultural backgrounds need to have opportunities to share their individual likes and culture so cultural proficiency can be learned

As with any subject area, learning to respect others has its ups and downs. Therefore, a skilled teacher must know how to encourage discussion and sharing when resistance occurs. The more opportunities that students have to share knowledge and feelings, the easier it is to deal with unforeseen contentious situations. Any person, child or adult, can better weather negative situations if he or she has a reservoir of positive feelings.

When a student is able to learn courtesy and respect as habits in a social setting, she or he can more easily become an empathetic person. When there is respect for others notwithstanding external differences, a student can better care for the plight of others. When you know someone is hurting, you hurt along with them. When a friend is injured or loses something or someone that they like or love, a kind, courteous, respectful person feels saddened for them and seeks to comfort them. Conversely, when someone we know is elated, we are happy for them. Empathy is caring for others and must start as youngsters. We all know that it becomes more and more difficult to change behaviors as we age. Unfortunately, students who don't learn to be empathetic usually do not have a very pleasant adulthood nor do the people associated with them. One trait that most sociopaths have is a lack of empathy. Being sad or happy for others, even those you do not know very well is a manifestation of respect in a tangible way.

Empathy has the unique quality of bringing forth random acts of kindness. Equated to the cognitive domain, this would be the application level. A caring, empathetic person values doing random acts of kindness. Empathy can be shown by helping another student with a difficult task, writing a thank you letter or letter of condolence, or merely paying someone an unsolicited compliment. Random acts of kindness transcend the mere talk and understanding of kindness into kindness actions. As a school principal, I was constantly looking for random acts of kindness whether in the classroom or on the playground. Just as students can exhibit random acts of kindness, so too can the adults who supervise them. At the end of every school day during a brief period of evaluation and reflection before dismissal, the question could be asked of any class if they noted any random acts of kindness during the day. This can be done without necessarily naming the person who did the kind act. The beauty of acts of kindness is that they provide their own rewards without the need for compliments. When you end a school day on a positive note, it is much easier to start the next day and so on in a positive manner.

Finally, the highest level in our social domain taxonomy hierarchy is living a life of kindness and goodness. The ultimate goal of the taxonomy is to lead a life that demonstrates care for all people. We do good deeds not for personal recognition but rather for the inner satisfaction that acts of kindness bring to us as its own reward and what it does for the recipient. We rarely know how kindness and goodness affect recipients or observers; however, we do have an indicator when a smile begets someone else's smile. In a religious realm, this might be called leading a saintly life. This ideal may sound somewhat naive and simplistic; however, if the alternative is a self centered, dog-eat-dog type of world, what ideal would you rather have? As a school teacher and principal, my goal was to have the best learning situation possible for all of my students. Social learning had to be at the core of my ideal school. All students regardless of family background, demographic circumstances or any other extraneous attribute needed to be in a caring environment. Where else should we start to develop caring students than in their school? Students caring for other students, families caring for other families just might grow to be all people caring for all other people.

The concept of "it takes a village to nurture children" certainly applies to all domains of learning, but especially the social domain. Just as it is counterproductive for parents not to be on the same page when raising their children, so, too, with social learning in the school setting. If a classroom teacher is promoting kindness, but other adults on staff are not, the student is receiving a mixed message. Therefore, a school wide kindness policy needs to be implemented for every adult on campus to use. All students at all grade levels, as well as all staff members, need to use courtesy phrases when making requests of students or adults. Children on the playground and in the cafeteria can practice courtesy when receiving their lunch trays or playing games. Staff members modeling positive courtesy in all aspects of teacher/student interactions is critical for learning kindness. Children also need to learn that we don't treat an unkindness with a reactionary unkind act. Children need to be taught that it is appropriate to say "Please stop!" when someone is harassing them. If the perpetrator of the harassment does not stop but persists, the child has the right to ask any supervising adult for assistance. During a counseling session with a child who persists in harassing others, the child needs to learn the inappropriateness of the action and in turn needs to learn that an unkind act can be corrected by a tangible act of kindness such as writing a letter of apology or in the case of young children drawing a picture for the person to whom they were unkind. In other words, learn to correct an unkind act with a corresponding act of kindness to rebuild respect. Parents many times will say that they teach their child to hit back if hit, and my response would be that in our school that is not acceptable. Therefore, parent education regarding the kindness policy is critical to its success. If altercations happen to us as we get immersed in the big, wide world, we have police and a legal system to assist us so that we don't have to be unkind in return. In this way, we foster kindness and hopefully eliminate altercations which can result in unnecessary injuries or even death

Schools are our magnificent institutions for learning and for teaching children how to cope in a world we know can be very unkind at times. Teaching social skills in order to lead a life of kindness and goodness is a noble calling. As the song says, Let there be peace on earth and let it begin with me.

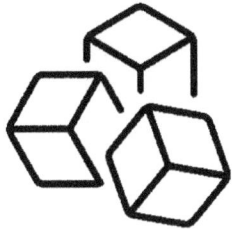

Chapter 6 – Emotional/Spiritual Domain

The emotional/spiritual domain like the social domain tends to be a forgotten domain in teacher planning. In educational research the emotional domain is also known as a spiritual domain. However, the spiritual domain is often referred to as the domain rooted in religious beliefs which keeps it from educational discussions in public education due to the separation of church and state. This is especially true in the United States where the separation of church and state is constitutionally fundamental to the public school curriculum. However, while the spiritual domain can have a religious orientation, it is rooted in secular beliefs as well.

Spirituality is connected to what is discussed as the life force, God, a higher power or purpose according to *Great Mystery*, Tisdell (2003). It helps individuals to live at peace with themselves, to love God and their neighbor, and to live in harmony with the environment, John (2011). It gives a sense of wholeness and leads to spiritual being which is defined as "the affirmation of life in a relationship with God, self, community and environment that nurtures and celebrates wholeness" NICA (1975). Daniel Goleman popularized research into emotional intelligence by pointing out that emotional intelligence is the basic requirement for the appropriate use of cognitive intelligence. Later, many have made significant contributions to the field of spiritual intelligence with Zohar and Marshall (2000) defining it as: *The intelligence with which we address and solve problems of meaning and value, the intelligence with which we can place our actions and our lives in a wider, richer, meaning giving context and intelligence with which we can assess the one course of action or one life-path more meaningful than another, p.3.*

The taxonomy of emotional (spiritual) learning can be described as follows:

1. Image awareness and appreciation. The understanding that despite faults, each individual in society has worth and value. A positive image allows an individual to rise above temporary setbacks that occur during a lifetime and give a life a positive meaning. Individual accomplishments enhance the feeling of worth and the value of one's life. One life cannot encompass the whole of society so just as in cognitive learning where an individual selects a field of interest for in-depth analysis and study; self image awareness is usually manifested in one area. Self-worth is seen in positive parenting, caring for the sick, teaching others, any field that provides service to others or develops a product that enhances the quality of life for others. In other words, something that contributes to society where the greater society gives positive feedback for one's actions.

2. Love of others. It is often said that you can't truly love and appreciate others if you can't first love and appreciate yourself.

The spiritual commandment of God is rooted in the belief that a person must love God and love their "neighbor" as themselves. Inherent in true love is respect, compassion and joy. Love also means giving to others not taking. Hopefully, when true love is shared, the person being loved is also giving love in return.

3. Love of Nature. Life as we know it on earth cannot exist without our natural surroundings. The awareness that all people on earth need to nurture and protect our environment if life on earth is to exist is intrinsic to our spiritual/emotional growth. Balancing progress and life needs with the need to sustain clean air, water, plant growth and natural resource limitations is part of a belief system about nature and its fragility. Again, it is a common need for all mankind, a shared need.

4. Transcendent Beliefs. Inherent in all of mankind is wonder and curiosity. This is the basis for all scientific and social research. It is the belief that allows all people to be creative in art, music, literature and any other creative endeavor. It is also the belief that life itself has meaning beyond our human existence. We often refer to lives lived beyond our personal needs as a "saintly" life. Also, the belief in a higher power, God, is rooted in transcendental belief.

5. Leadership: Encouraging others to lead a life of purpose and service to community is a natural outgrowth of a positive spiritual belief. This is the main reason why teaching is such a noble profession. However, spiritual/emotional leadership is truly only accomplished through modeling. Any individual person who models positive values such as kindness, sharing, forgiveness, caring for others and any other societal value is demonstrating spiritual and emotional leadership.

As a society, we attempt to codify the emotional/spiritual domain in terms of ethical behaviors. We develop the ethic of law, medicine, government and many other endeavors. Defining the right way to conduct ourselves in society. In human history we have seen what happens to society when ethic is negative and based on power, greed, superiority and egotistical narcissism. Power can corrupt society if a society weakens its spiritual/emotional belief system.

Public and private education has long attempted to include self image awareness, respect for others and ecology into the school curriculum. However, as with affective, psychomotor and social learning, it can be limited due to time constraints of the school day and year, as well as the over-emphasis on the cognitive and somewhat the psychomotor domains. The challenge in teaching is how can all domains of learning be synthesized into teaching to the whole student. Also, how can all domains of learning be outsourced to families and the greater culture so that everyone in society becomes a teacher by modeling appropriate behaviors. This is obviously a daunting task or we would already be living in a perfect society, a Garden of Eden. But, we have so many examples throughout history of individuals making a difference and collectively achieving cultural greatness. Goodness begets goodness. Kindness begets kindness, caring begets caring. And love begets love. Doing good things for the right reasons of giving, for giving's sake, does allow any individual to grow and prosper while also helping the greater society do the same.

Religious Addendum for the spiritual domain:

As with the cognitive, affective, psychomotor and social domains of learning, the spiritual domain can also be categorized in a taxonomy of learned skill levels. The hierarchy levels could be knowledge, comprehension, application, synthesis, and evaluation similar to the cognitive domain levels but with spiritual specificity. For example, spiritual knowledge and comprehension come from spiritual sources such as the Bible, Torah, Koran and other religious texts and scholarly publications.

Application could be found in our beliefs, prayer, ministries, charitable works and social justice activities. Synthesis could be finding spiritual goodness, or God, in humanity, all aspects of our natural world and in our inner self. Evaluation could be found in tests of our beliefs such as our spiritual reactions to pain, suffering, humiliation and even death. Unfortunately, as with the other domain taxonomies, learning tends to stop at the levels of knowledge, comprehension, and some aspects of application such as prayer and beliefs. We have many models for synthesis and evaluation of the spiritual domain in the lives of saintly people and most importantly for Christians in the life of Jesus Christ. Jesus was the ultimate teacher in that his life modeled the highest levels of spiritual learning. How did he treat others based on his teachings? How did he deal with rejection, pain and suffering? And how did he deal with his death at the hands of others? Basically, reaching higher spiritual levels means creating goodness around us especially where it may not exist either within ourselves or in our community.

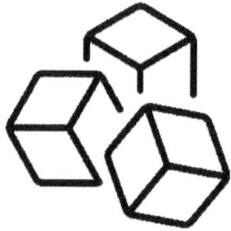

Chapter 7 – Integrating Domains of Learning

Time is always a major factor when planning any activity. As learning becomes more and more complex, the time needed to teach becomes less and less. The current political climate related to education has been dictating that cognitive skills are the priority in teaching; so, where does that leave the teaching related to the other four domains of learning. Educational budgets also reflect the dominance of the cognitive domain. When budget cuts need to be made by boards of education at the local level, it is usually at the expense of the arts, physical education and local school choice. Teaching to a national or state standardized test dictates that aspects of the cognitive domain be dominant. And it also means that lower level cognitive taxonomies of knowledge and comprehension are valued much more than higher level taxonomy skills such as analysis, synthesis and evaluation. I would submit that standardized tests not only greatly curtail the affective, psychomotor, social and emotional/spiritual domains but also dumb down the cognitive domain as well. Where is the creativity in the standardized test?

In the mid-1990s when standardized tests based on a standards based curriculum were being implemented in California, the State Department of Education authorized the development of the California Achievement Test for selected elementary, middle school and high school grade levels that was based on the writing process. Prompts were developed that guided students at those grade levels to write a personal report based on concepts that they had learned with their personal conclusions. These reports were "graded" for content and scholarship by teams of local teacher evaluators on a scale from outstanding to needs improvement in specific curricular areas. This CAT testing lasted for one year and was then abandoned because the use of trained teacher evaluators in each school district was considered to be too expensive when compared to bubble-in machine-scored tests. Also, in the 1990s student journaling was made mandatory in some school districts as a way to track student learning with high school graduation and intermediate promotions based partially on the journal content. The journals reflected not only cognitive learning but affective, psychomotor, social and emotional comments as well. Unfortunately for journaling, the journals took teacher time which took teachers away from standardized test preparation which was given much more weight in the overall evaluation process at the state, local and national levels. These two attempts to personalize the evaluation process and include all domains of learning were scraped due to budgetary reasons. Just think where the education process would be if the money spent on evaluation had gone to train teachers in the process and personalize the student learning in all domains instead of paying corporations to machine score impersonal tests in limited cognitive domain areas.

With all domains of learning still needed for the educational development of all children at all grade levels, the question then becomes, how can a teacher or parent incorporate all domains in the development of a whole learning process for every student The answer is the same as it has always been; outstanding teachers who are trained to understand the importance of all learning domains integrate their curriculum. There are many examples from great teachers at all grade levels of integrated learning. But, great teachers need great training during the teacher training process. Unfortunately, teacher training college years and activities have been cut for many years. Schools of education which used to require two full semesters of student teaching, now only require six to eight week sessions. This shortened time for actual in-person student teaching does not allow prospective teachers to fully develop a semester plan for student learning and the time to learn how to integrate all domains of learning. Therefore, the needed curricular training is becoming the responsibility of local districts and individual schools to implement meaningful staff development opportunities for all teachers. Peer training is the only method readily available and it is limited by local budgets. The few days a year set aside for staff training in local schools is limited and must be used judiciously.

In my experience as a school administrator evaluating teachers, whether new to the profession or experienced, the major weakness that I observed was the evaluation process for daily achievement and integrated domain learning. Most teachers did not understand the value of taking ten minutes at the end of the school day to discuss with their students what had been learned that day and what it would lead to the next day. It was also a time to celebrate successes and appreciate the class community. This was also a time for students to write daily comments in their personal journals which could be shared daily with their parents. When time is limited during the school day, teachers tend to make assignments rather than discuss assignments while remembering the need for motivation. When teachers need to cover a stated curriculum of topics within a certain time frame, they then tend to eliminate meaningful discussion and rely on rote learning

Teacher training, whether in the college setting or local school staff development, needs to inspire teachers to integrate all domains in their teaching by the way they develop their lesson plans. The seven step lesson plan that was first introduced by Madeline Hunter at UCLA is still a useful guide in lesson planning. It has always incorporated motivation or prior knowledge which is based on prior successes, and personal evaluation as part of the step process.

It is my great hope that anyone reading this book, especially teachers, would engage in conversations with friends and colleagues about ways in which they can integrate domains of learning in whatever teaching they do. Teachers at all grade levels should be using staff development time to assess their lesson planning to enrich it. Parents can discuss with other parents ways in which they have fostered domain learning with their children. It has been said that all adults are teachers and that is true, but before you can be a teacher, you need to be a learner. In our current information age where knowledge and discourse can be shared by millions almost instantaneously, there is no excuse for not learning, sharing and synthesizing knowledge. We are all lifelong learners and teachers.

Let me start the discussion of integrated domain learning with a few examples:

1. The Writing Process: Given a prompt such as "Write about a random act of kindness that you have done or experienced," a student in preschool could make an illustration or write a dictated story, an elementary student could write a simple paragraph with an illustration, a middle or high school student could write a

comprehensive report and a college student could write a term paper. The illustration or text is cognitive, the choice is affective, the prompt has both a social meaning and caring component, and the emotional/spiritual is about personal values. When the completed illustration or text is shared in class or published, the illustrator or writer should receive applause and recognition for image development. The kindness that was shared is also a model for the listeners or readers to follow as well.

2. Playground Sports: Teaching competitive games from kickball in elementary school to softball and baseball in middle and high school can teach multiple domains. The most obvious is the psychomotor domain where students, especially small children can be taught physical skills like eye/hand coordination and muscle development through throwing, catching, hitting and kicking. Cognitive skills like reading rules are inherent in learning games. With practice, children can learn to expand their skills and improvise. Strategy and critical thinking become a part of any sport. Success in sports can contribute to the affective domain and create lifelong healthy interests. The social domain is an intrinsic part of sports because the required teamwork includes the appreciation for the achievements of others as well as self. Self-image in the emotional/spiritual domain comes with enjoyment and success and being part of the natural environment.

3. Reading for Enjoyment: The basic skill of reading is developed through storytelling and story reading. Children's literature encompasses everything from simple picture books to novels. Affective choice is inherent in the enjoyment of reading. Just like in the writing process, selection is the key to lifelong reading. Every school classroom at every grade level should have a classroom library with at least five times the number of books as students in the class on a variety of topics and reading levels. If children read for enjoyment and share their choices with their

classmates, they are contributing to the affective and social domains. Sharing develops emotional self image when applause is given to the sharer.

4. Math Games: Mathematics from counting to higher level skills are a part of many games that children enjoy. When students create relationship cards for basic math processes like addition/subtraction and multiplication/division, they can better understand the underlying concepts. Creating Napier Rods for multiplication can also involve psychomotor skills like sawing, sanding and measuring. Handwriting, whether numbers or letters, is also a psychomotor skill. Creating math contests is a social activity. Incremental successes in learning math concepts create self image building in the emotional domain. Playing games like Monopoly is both cognitive and social. Teaching children to play chess creates opportunities for abstract knowledge and strategy to be developed through analysis. Abstract art activities can bring concepts in geometry to life.

5. Art and Music: Self-expression can be found in writing, reading, sports and games, but it is most readily found in art and music. When children or adults express themselves in art and music which also includes dance, they are integrating cognitive skills with affective choice, social skills of sharing, psychomotor skills through movement and implement manipulation, and of course self-image development and the appreciation of others. All five domains can be found in art and music if students are given the time to develop those interests. Students exposed to art and music, just like when they enjoy reading by being exposed to stories, is always the first step in the education process. A student cannot appreciate what they have never known. Integrating art and music into the reading and math curriculum can enhance not detract from the core curricular subjects. As a teacher, I found that even the students who struggled with most reading were able to

read music and perform at a high level. Students who struggled with mathematics could learn the rhythm and beat of music and its mathematical quality.

6. Vocabulary Development: As I discussed earlier in this text, vocabulary development is one of the keys to discreet learning. The vocabulary that is introduced for each lesson can be included in a daily journal or individual subject dictionary. Learning to spell words that need to be used by students during their lessons or words developed by students with prefixes, suffixes and tenses continues to make learning meaningful and not a rote activity. Creating vocabulary games enhances the affective, social and emotional/spiritual domains as well

7. Questioning: Questioning for higher levels of thinking as well as for basic understanding and knowledge is also a key component of teaching. Students at all levels can learn to ask a variety of questions related to any subject area. In addition, the higher levels of questioning acknowledge individual student understanding within the concept that none of us is as smart as all of us. Higher-level questions, by their very nature, encompass the affective, social, and emotional/spiritual domains. Basic knowledge questions include yes/no questions and who, what, where, and when questions. Higher-level questions include how and why questions. Students can create their own questions for lessons that they are learning and evaluate the level of the question with all questions being acceptable.

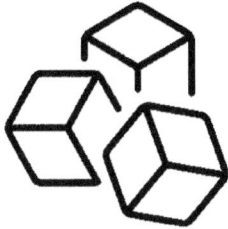

Chapter 8 – Conclusion

Becoming familiar with domains of learning is the key to the teaching process and the development of students as lifelong learners. All human beings whether young or old, strive for enjoyment and fulfillment. What better way to achieve enjoyment and fulfillment than by personal lifelong learning. As an adult, where did you receive the input for your lifelong learning? Do you like golf as an adult because you were introduced to the game at a young age and enjoyed the experience? Have you used oral communication to discuss your round of golf in the clubhouse with friends? Wasn't your score based on mathematics? When you played a good round, did it enhance your self image? As an adult, do you enjoy a career or do you merely go to work to earn money? We tend to enjoy work and make careers out of work when it brings us satisfaction and positive responses in addition to earning money. Of course we all want to earn as much money as possible, but the reason we want the money is usually so that we can make more personal choices during our lifetime. The five domains of learning will always be a part of what we do in our daily lives. In order to truly be our best selves, we need to continue to develop higher order taxonomy skills in the five domains which start when we are young and in school. The higher taxonomy skills in the cognitive and psychomotor domains help us to become true experts in our careers. The higher taxonomy skills in the affective domain help us fully enjoy our careers. The higher taxonomy skills in the social and emotional/spiritual domains allow us to grow beyond self interest, egotism and narcissism into caring, empathetic and socially responsible member of society and become a true leader. We may respect everyone, but we revere those who have also led an exemplary life that has served as a model for all mankind. Teaching is one of the noblest of professions because teachers have the ability through their teaching to help all students become the best version of themselves.

Bibliography

Hunter, Madeline (1982), Hunter, Robin (Revised 2004). Mastery TeachingIncreasing Instructional Effectiveness in Elementary and Secondary Schools. Thousand OaksCorwin Press

Bloom, B.S. (1956). Taxonomy of Educational Objectives, Handbook I: The Cognitive Domain. New YorkDavid McKay Co., Inc.

Dave, R. (1970). Psychomotor Levels in R.J. Armstrong (edDeveloping and Writing Behavioral Objectives. Tucson, ArizonaEducational Innovators Press

Harrow, A.J. (1972). A Taxonomy of the Psychomotor Domain. New York: David McKay Co., Inc.

Krathwohl, D.R., Bloom, B.S., and Masia, B.B. (1973Taxonomy of Educational Objectives, The Classification of Educational Goals, Handbook IIAffective Domain. New York: David McKay Co., Inc.

Lindsey, R.B., Robins, K.N. and Terrell, R.D. (1999). Cultural Proficiency: A Manual for School Leaders. Thousand OaksCorwin Press, Inc.

John, F. (2011). The Four Domains ModelConnecting Spirituality, Health and Well-being. Religions, 2(1), 17-28.

Mathew, P. (2008). Education: The Means to Divinity, In Building a Culture of Peace for a Civil Society - Proceedings of the 12th World Conference on Education. Manila, Philippines.

National Interfaith Coalition on Aging, NICA (1975). Spiritual Well-being: A Definition. Athens, Georgia, USA: NICA

Tisdell, E. (2003). Exploring Spirituality and Culture in Adult and Higher EducationSan FranciscoJossey-Bass

Zohar, D. (2004). Spiritual Capital: Wealth We Can Live ByLondonBloomsbury

Zohar, D. and Marshall, I. (2000). SQ, Spiritual Intelligence: The Ultimate Intelligence. London: Bloomsbury

About the Author

Dan Basalone was an elementary classroom teacher, gifted/enrichment program teacher, Title I intergroup relations advisor, Title I school coordinator, elementary school assistant principal and principal, and director of professional development in the Los Angeles Unified School District over a forty year career. He served as a principal in five culturally distinct schools where he had the unique opportunity to put into practice what he had learned as a training teacher for California State University - Los Angeles and as an intergroup relations advisor. In addition to his work in LAUSD, he also served as associate professor of education for National University and clinical professor of educational administration at both California State University - Los Angeles and Dominguez Hills.

Upon retirement, he served as director of the educational administration program at Mount Saint Mary's University in Los Angeles. He received his BS degree in social studies, science and education from the University of Southern California and his MS degree in urban education and school administration from Mount Saint Mary's College.

At any level of education, teaching and learning is as noble as the values that we impart to our students.

www.ingramcontent.com/pod-product-compliance
Lightning Source LLC
Chambersburg PA
CBHW041153110526
44590CB00027B/4218